Peter

A model for following Jesus

By Tim Sawyer

Peter: A model for following Jesus

Copyright © 2016 by Sawyer Publications

All rights reserved. No part of this book may be reproduced in any form without permission in writing from the author. Reviewers may quote brief passages in reviews.

Disclaimer and FTC Notice

No part of this publication may be reproduced or transmitted in any form or by any means, mechanical or electronic, including photocopying or recording, or by any information storage and retrieval system, or transmitted by email without permission in writing from the publisher.

While all attempts have been made to verify the information provided in this publication, neither the author nor the publisher assumes any responsibility for errors, omissions, or contrary interpretations of the subject matter herein.

Neither the author nor the publisher assumes any responsibility or liability whatsoever on the behalf of the purchaser or reader of these materials. Any perceived slight of any individual or organization is purely unintentional.

Table of Contents

How to use this book 5

Introduction 6

Chapter 1 - Early ministry of Jesus 9

Chapter 2 - Later ministry of Jesus 29

Chapter 3 - Death of Jesus 49

Chapter 4 - Resurrection of Jesus 65

Chapter 5 - Church launch 79

Chapter 6 - Church outreach 99

Chapter 7 - New Testament books 117

Leader's Guide 125

Acknowledgments 130

Dedicated to Sherwood & Ruth Sawyer

How to use this book

The purpose of this book is to help you deepen your relationship with God. The process is simple.

Think about these Bible stories. Open your mind to what God is saying. Let the Bible impact you.

Read the biblical scene described in a paragraph. Then you can respond to the questions that follow.

As you answer those questions, or discuss them in a group, you may come up with more questions.

For example: What did Jesus mean? Why did Jesus do that? If I were Peter, how might I respond?

Scripture references are provided for each scene in case you want to do more personal study.

The advantage of doing an individual Bible study is that you can deal with private issues.

The advantage of doing a group Bible study is that you progress more quickly in your walk of faith.

Group discussions help you grow. They bring out new ideas that you may not think of by yourself.

God uses those around you to encourage you and to help you with changes you may wish to make. You may be the person God uses to help others.

Introduction

Simon the Rock. That's what Jesus called him. We call him Peter. We can only look at a person on the outside. Jesus looks on the inside. Jesus sees what we are, our failures, our flaws, and by faith our fabulous futures!

Jesus said, "Follow me." How do we do that? What does that mean? This New Testament guide helps you figure that out.

I wrote this as a Bible discussion guide for my small group. Personally, I want to follow the Lord faithfully. Some days I do. Other days I fall flat on my face. Thankfully, God and my small group love me anyway.

This book examines 51 scenes from the life of Peter. I paraphrase in my own words what is going on in each biblical scene. Scripture references allow you to look up the details more fully if you wish.

200 questions are provided as tools to deepen your faith. These conversation starters help you discuss, ponder, or share your thoughts. The goal of the questions is to help you feel what it was like to follow Jesus, like Peter did.

I love small groups. A book like this allows you to just show up and participate. Have fun and learn.

My plan is to read the scene, ask the questions and let friends share. You can follow Jesus and grow closer to him and each other at the same time.

In my lifetime I have read the Bible all the way through many times in several translations. In the 1970s I earned a degree in Ancient Languages. Over the years I translated many biblical books from the original Greek into English.

Before I retired from 26 years of ministry, people often asked me, "Which English translation of the Bible is the best?" My answer is, "The translation that you actually read!"

In 2016 I am reading the Sawyer translation. No, it's not mine. Leicester Ambrose Sawyer translated the New Testament rather literally in 1858. That's what I am reading this year. But enough about me.

Let's watch Peter follow Jesus. Maybe we can pick up some pointers for our own lives.

Chapter 1 - Early ministry of Jesus

Lamb of God

Fishers of men

Mother-in-law

Disciples sent out

Who touched me?

Jairus' daughter

Walk on water

Disciples turn back

Feeding 5000

Lamb of God

John 1:35-42

Andrew and another disciple came to hear John the Baptist preach. They heard John say that Jesus is the Lamb of God, which is the Messiah or Christ. Then these two disciples began to follow Jesus. They spent the rest of the day with him. Soon after, Andrew told his brother Simon about Jesus. When he saw Simon, Jesus called him "Cephas". (In their Aramaic language, "Cephas" is a form of the word for rock. The New Testament Greek word for rock is petra, leading to the English name "Peter".)

1. What do you think prompted John the Baptist to use the term Lamb of God?

2. What influence do you suppose John the Baptist had on his disciples?

3. How do you imagine the actions of Andrew influenced his brother Simon?

4. If you were Simon Peter, how would you feel about being called a rock?

Fishers of men

Luke 5:1-11; Matthew 4:18-20

Crowds gathered near the Sea of Galilee, also called the Sea of Gennesaret. Jesus saw two fishing boats. One belonged to James and John, and the other to Peter and Andrew. The men were washing their nets after a failed night of fishing. Jesus climbed into Peter's boat and taught those along the shore. When he finished, Jesus told Peter to take the boat out to deeper water and let down his nets. Peter objected but complied. Suddenly their nets were full of fish. They had to call for James and John to help. Peter fell down at the feet of Jesus and said, "Get away from me. I am a sinful man." Jesus replied, "Don't be afraid. You know how to fish. Follow me and learn how to fish for men." And so, they followed Jesus.

1. Why do you think crowds were following Jesus?

2. What would you think if Jesus asked you to go out into deeper water and throw down your nets?

3. If you were Peter, why would you be bothered by your own sinfulness?

4. How does the reply of Jesus encourage you?

Mother-in-law

Matthew 8:14-17; Mark 1:29-31; Luke 4:38-39

After Jesus preached the Sermon on the Mount, he came down into Capernaum with his disciples and went into the synagogue. When Jesus finished there, Peter and Andrew invited Jesus down the street to their family home. Their close friends James and John came along. Inside the house, they told Jesus that Peter's mother-in-law was bedridden and sick with a high fever. Jesus saw her, rebuked the fever, and took her by the hand. Instantly she was healed. Then she got up and waited on them.

1. If you were Peter, why would you bring Jesus into your home?

2. What does this passage reveal to you about Jesus' power?

3. When someone is sick, what circumstances make you want to tell Jesus about their need for healing?

4. If you were Peter's mother-in-law, how might you react if Jesus healed you?

Disciples sent out

Matthew 9:37-38; 10:1-2; Mark 3:16; Luke 6:13-15

Jesus told the disciples to ask the Lord for workers to go out into the harvest. Then Jesus called a small group of twelve. The first two he chose were the brothers Peter and Andrew. As disciples the twelve followed Jesus and learned about God. These disciples were designated as apostles to be sent out on a missionary tour. Jesus gave them authority and a spiritual mission to heal the sick and deal with demons. The disciples followed the instructions of Jesus by going out to meet needs.

1. How would you feel if you were chosen to be a disciple of Jesus?

2. What do you see as the main responsibilities of these apostles?

3. What reaction do you imagine the people had to the apostles and their ministry?

4. What impact do you think their mission had on the ministry of Jesus?

Who touched me?

Luke 8:40-48

When Jesus returned from a trip, Jairus intercepted Jesus to bring him to his home. A woman there in the crowd had been bleeding for 12 years. Even the most expensive doctors could not cure her. As Jesus jostled through the crowd, she reached out and touched the edge of his clothes. Immediately her bleeding stopped. Then Jesus asked, "Who touched me?" Everyone denied it. Peter explained that with people crowding all around, it could have been anyone. But Jesus replied that he felt the power surge. The woman was afraid. She admitted that she had touched him. Jesus declared her faith had healed her and sent her away in peace.

1. If you were that woman, what would you be thinking before you touched Jesus?

2. If you were Peter, what would you think when Jesus asked such a question?

3. What do you suppose the woman felt when she realized she was healed?

4. Why do you think Jesus called her out in front of everyone?

Jairus' daughter

Luke 8:49-56; Mark 5:21-43

Jerusalem had their temple. Other towns had local synagogues for Sabbath worship. One synagogue official named Jairus had stopped Jesus on his way into town. He begged Jesus to come heal his only daughter. The 12 year old child was deathly ill. They headed toward the man's house, but Jesus was delayed. First there was the woman who touched Jesus. Then they got a report that the man's daughter had died. They told Jairus not to trouble the teacher anymore. Jesus turned to Jairus and told him not to be afraid. Just believe and the girl will be fine. They kept walking. When they got to the house, Jesus kept everyone back. He took Peter, James, John, and the girl's parents into the house. Then Jesus healed the girl.

1. Why do you think many Jews worshipped at synagogues instead of the temple?

2. What do you suspect local synagogue officials thought about Jesus?

3. If you were Jairus, what might you have been thinking that day?

4. Why do you think Jesus only let a few people come into the house?

Walk on water

Matthew 14:25-33

Jesus put his disciples in a boat and sent them across the Sea of Galilee. Then he went up into a mountain to pray by himself. Early in the morning the wind and waves caused problems for those in the boat. Before dawn Jesus came walking on the water. When they saw him, they were afraid. They didn't know who or what they saw. Jesus spoke to reassure them. Peter asked if he could meet Jesus walking on the water. "Come," Jesus said. Peter climbed out of the boat and walked on the water. When Peter noticed the strong wind, he became afraid and down he sank. Jesus grabbed him. He asked Peter why he had such little faith. When they climbed into the boat, the wind stopped. After that, they proclaimed Jesus to be the Son of God.

1. Why do you think Jesus sent his disciples across the water?

2. When have you been too quick to volunteer?

3. Why do you suppose Peter was able to walk on the water?

4. Moments later, what do you think caused Peter to sink?

Disciples turn back

John 6:66-69

Many people liked to listen to Jesus when he taught at the synagogue in Capernaum. Then one day Jesus said that he was the living bread who came down from heaven. Jesus told them that they would have to eat his flesh and drink his blood. Only those who believe in him can go to heaven. The doubters said, "He didn't come from heaven. We know his parents!" After this, many disciples deserted Jesus. So he turned to the original twelve. Jesus asked them if they wanted to leave too. Peter answered, "Lord, where could we go? You're the only one who offers the words of eternal life. We believe you are the Holy One of God."

1. What do you think caused some people to doubt Jesus and his teaching?

2. Why do you suppose it was a problem for them that they knew his parents?

3. If you were one of the original twelve disciples, why might you be more likely to believe?

4. What do you imagine the disciples believed about Jesus?

Feeding the 5000

John 6:1-13; Matthew 14:13-21; Mark 6:30-44; Luke 9:10-17

Jesus went up on a hillside near the Sea of Galilee. Then he sat down with his disciples. Five thousand people showed up, because many of them had seen his miracles of healing. As the crowd arrived Jesus spent time teaching. After a while they got hungry. The disciples told Jesus to send the people away so they could find food. Instead, Jesus asked Philip, "Where are we going to buy food to feed this crowd?" (Jesus already knew what would happen.) Philip said it would be very expensive, even if they could. But Peter's brother Andrew had found a boy with five loaves of bread and two fish. So Jesus told his disciples to have the people sit down on the grass. Jesus broke up the food. The disciples distributed the pieces to the crowd until everyone was full. They collected 12 baskets of leftovers.

1. If you had come to see Jesus that day, what would you expect to happen?

2. Why do you think Jesus asked Philip where they could buy food?

3. Why do you suppose Peter's brother Andrew got involved?

4. Why do you think the feeding of the 5000 is told in all four gospels?

Prayer concerns

Prayer:

Lord, thank you for being a God of surprises. Your power is more than I can understand. Help me to set aside the distractions of life. What do you want to say to me? Right now I will be silent and listen.

(Pause the prayer for a moment and listen to God.)

You care about everyone in my life. I am amazed. Give me a heart for those in need around me as I seek to follow Jesus.

Amen.

Chapter 2 - Later ministry of Jesus

Clean and unclean

Peter's confession

Get behind me, Satan!

The Transfiguration

Repeated forgiveness

Watch and be ready

We left everything

Fig tree withered

End time signs

Clean and unclean

Matthew 15:15

Jewish religious leaders had traditional rules for ceremonial washing before they ate. The disciples did not follow those rules. When the Pharisees complained, Jesus called them hypocrites. Then he contrasted their outward practice with a person's inward faith by using a parable. Peter asked Jesus to explain the parable. Jesus said the Pharisees were like plants that God had not planted. "Leave them because they are like blind guides." It is not what goes into the person that makes a person unclean. Impurity is what comes out of the person, like evil thoughts and bad behavior. Those things come from the heart.

1. Can you think of any rules that people follow as part of their religion? Name some.

2. Do you think a church should have rules? Why? or Why not?

3. If you were Peter, how would you react to what Jesus was saying in this passage?

4. What types of behavior do you think seem most important to Jesus?

Peter's confession

Matthew 16:13-20; Mark 8:29-30; Luke 9:18-22

Jesus asked his disciples, "Who do people say that I am?" They gave him many answers, including famous prophets from the past. So he asked, "What about you? Who do you say that I am?" Peter said, "You are the Christ (the Anointed Messiah), the Son of the living God." Jesus replied, "Blessed are you Simon, son of Jonah. My father God in heaven revealed that to you. And you are Peter, and on this rock I will build my church." Then Jesus told his disciples not to tell anyone that he is the Christ.

1. What are some incorrect statements about Jesus that you have heard people say?

2. Why do you think Jesus is so concerned with what his disciples believe?

3. In what context have you heard Jesus referred to as a rock?

4. What do you think Jesus meant by his comment "upon this rock I will build my church"?

Get behind me, Satan!

Matthew 16:21-28; Mark 8:31-33

Jesus explained to his disciples that He must go to Jerusalem to be killed and to rise again on the third day. Peter rebuked Jesus, "Never, Lord!" But Jesus reprimanded him, "You are following Satan's plan to trip me up!" Peter only looked at the situation from a human point of view and not God's point of view. Jesus commanded, "Deny yourself, take up your cross and follow me." He added that to save your life you must lose it. Everything that you can imagine is of less value than your own soul.

1. Why do you think Jesus told them he would rise on the third day?

2. Why do you think that the words "Never" and "Lord" do not fit together well?

3. How much to you think Satan knew about God's plan to have Jesus die and rise again?

4. What does it mean for you to take up your cross and follow Jesus?

The Transfiguration

Luke 9:28-36; Matthew 17:1-13; Mark 9:2-13; 2 Peter 1:16-21

Jesus took Peter, James and John up a mountain to pray. During the prayer meeting the disciples were drowsy. Then suddenly the face of Jesus changed and his clothes turned bright white. Moses and Elijah appeared and were talking with Jesus about his upcoming death in Jerusalem. Now fully awake, the disciples saw the whole thing. Peter said it was awesome to be there. He volunteered to build three shelters for them, not understanding the situation. A cloud covered the disciples, causing them to be afraid. They heard a voice. "This is my chosen Son. Listen to him!" Everything cleared, and Jesus was standing there by himself. The disciples did not speak about this to anyone.

1. Why do you suppose Jesus only took with him Peter, James and John?

2. What does the transfiguration make you think about Jesus?

3. If you were Peter, why would you volunteer to put up shelters?

4. Why do you think the voice spoke to the three disciples?

Repeated forgiveness

Matthew 18:15-22

Jesus taught that if your brother sins against you, go and work it out. If you can't, then take someone else along. If you still can't, get help from the church. And if that doesn't work, treat him like an unbeliever. The goal is to be in agreement with other believers. So Peter asked, "How many times do I have to forgive my brother when he sins against me? Maybe seven times?" Jesus said, "No, that's not enough. Try seventy times seven."

1. Why does Jesus want you to work out your differences?

2. When have you successfully managed to improve a difficult relationship?

3. What do you think the church could do to help out when one Christian sins against another?

4. Why do you suppose Peter wanted to limit the number to seven times?

Watch and be ready

Luke 12:35-48

Jesus told a parable about a master going away. When the master returns, the good servants are ready to open the door for him, even if he shows up in the middle of the night. Servants must watch and be ready because they don't know when he is coming. Peter asked if the parable was for them or others. Jesus asked them questions. Then he added that more will be expected from the ones who have been given more.

1. Why do you suppose Peter wanted to know who the parable was for?

2. What are some bad things that you know that believers sometimes do?

3. What are some good things that you know that believers sometimes fail to do?

4. How can you determine how much the Lord expects of you?

We left everything

Matthew 19:16-30; Mark 10:21-31; Luke 18:22-30

A wealthy young man asked how he could have eternal life. Jesus said, "Sell your possessions, give to the poor, and follow me. Your treasure will be in heaven." The young man couldn't handle that and left. Jesus told his disciples that it is harder for a rich person to get to heaven than for a camel to go through the eye of a needle. They asked, "Who then can be saved?" Peter said, "We have left everything to follow you!" Then Jesus said that those who have left houses and family for God will inherit 100 times more.

1. What does the young man's question tell you about being rich?

2. Why do you suppose that some people think the rich may be closer to God?

3. Why do you think it is hard for some to trust in God instead of their wealth?

4. What kind of benefit can you imagine for those who have left everything for Jesus?

Fig tree withered

Mark 11:12-14, 20-25

The day after Palm Sunday, Jesus was hungry. When he left Bethany for their trip to Jerusalem, he saw a fig tree with leaves. Then Jesus went over to check out the tree. But there was nothing on it, because it wasn't yet the season for figs. So Jesus cursed a fig tree saying that it would never bear fruit again. The next day on their trip into the city, Peter remarked that the tree had withered. Jesus told them that if they believed and did not doubt, then whatever they ask in prayer would happen.

1. What does his physical hunger tell you about Jesus?

2. Why do you think Jesus cursed the tree when it didn't have figs?

3. Why do you suppose Peter was amazed that the fig tree had withered?

4. How does faith affect God's answer to your prayers?

End time signs

Mark 13:1-37; Matthew 24:1-51; Luke 21:1-38

As they left the temple, the disciples discussed the impressive stones used in its construction. Jesus told them that every one of those stones would be toppled. They crossed over to the Mount of Olives. Peter, James, John and Andrew sat alone alongside Jesus as they looked back at the city. They asked him when all these things would happen. What would be signs that the temple is about to be destroyed? Jesus compared the fall of Jerusalem to the final end times. Jesus told them that the gospel must first be preached to all nations.

1. Why might you value an impressive building that is used for worship?

2. Why do you suppose Jesus did not seem awe-struck with these temple stones?

3. Why do you think these four disciples wanted to be alone with Jesus?

4. How do you think the gospel will be preached to all nations?

Prayer concerns

Prayer

Dear Lord, You are the God of wisdom. You know all truth. Your word is truth.

Forgive me for my foolishness. Help me to forgive others as often as I need too.

Teach me to know more of you. Guide me to walk in your ways.

In Jesus' name,

Amen.

Chapter 3 - Death of Jesus

Last Supper preparation

Jesus washes feet

Betrayal predicted

Gethsemane

Ear cut off

Peter's denial

Last Supper preparation

Luke 22:7-12; Matthew 26:17-19; Mark 14:12-16

The day arrived for the feast of the Unleavened Bread. Jesus sent Peter and John to make preparations to eat the Passover meal that night. They asked Jesus where he wanted them to set it up. He said that when they go into the city of Jerusalem, a man carrying a pitcher of water will meet them. Follow him home. Tell the man that the teacher needs his guestroom to celebrate the Passover with his disciples. Prepare the meal there.

1. Why do you think that celebrating the Passover would be important to them?

2. Why do you think Jesus chose Peter and John?

3. Why do you think Jesus chose that man's home?

4. What do you think the man thought about this request?

Jesus washes feet

John 13:2-9

During the Last Supper, Jesus took off his outer clothes and wrapped a towel around his waist. Jesus poured water into a basin and began to wash his disciples' feet. Peter resisted. Jesus told him he would understand later. Peter said, "No, you're not washing my feet." Jesus replied, "If I don't, then you are not one of my followers." Peter exclaimed, "Well then, wash everything!" Jesus said, "You don't need a bath. I have set an example for you. No servant is greater than his master. You will need to wash one another's feet and be blessed."

1. Why do you think Jesus chose this moment to wash the disciples' feet?

2. If you were Peter, how might you react to Jesus washing your feet?

3. What do you think this foot washing meant for the disciples?

4. What do you suppose foot washing would mean in the future for disciples?

Betrayal predicted

John 13:18-30; Matthew 26:20-25; Mark 14:17-21; Luke 22:21-23

Jesus became troubled in spirit. He predicted that one of the twelve disciples would betray him. The disciples looked at each other dumbfounded. They began to ask, "Am I the one?" Peter motioned to John, "Ask him which one he means." Jesus said, "It's the one to whom I give this piece of bread." Then he dipped the bread into a bowl and handed it to Judas Iscariot. Judas asked, "Surely you don't mean me?" Jesus said, "Yes, it's you. Now go do what you need to do." Judas got up and left. Since he was their treasurer, the disciples thought Judas was taking care of a financial matter for Jesus.

1. What do you think bothered Jesus most about the betrayal?

2. What do you suppose the disciples were thinking as they looked at each other?

3. Why do you think Peter's reaction is different from that of the other disciples?

4. What do you suppose Judas thought when Jesus handed him the bread?

Denial predicted

Matthew 26:31-35; Mark 14:27-31; Luke 22:31-38; John 13:31-38

Jesus told his disciples that he would be with them for just a little while longer. Then he was going away. Peter asked, "Lord, where are you going?" Jesus said, "Where I am going you cannot follow me now, but you will follow me later." But Peter protested, "Why can't I follow you now? Others may leave you, but I won't. I'm ready to die for you!" Jesus asked, "Are you really ready? Before the rooster crows in the morning, you will deny me three times." Then Jesus added, "I used to send you out without anything, and you were fine. But now you need to bring money and a sword." The disciples said, "We have two swords here," Jesus replied, "That's enough."

1. Why do you think Jesus told his disciples that he was going away?

2. What do you think is the most promising thing Jesus said here about Peter?

3. How do you think the other disciples reacted to the way Peter portrayed himself?

4. If you were Peter, how would you feel if Jesus predicted your denial?

Gethsemane

Matthew 26:36-46; Mark 14:32-42; John 17:1-26

They returned to the Mount of Olives where they had spent the night. Jesus stopped to pray at the foot of the hill, in the garden with the olive oil press called Gethsemane. Jesus felt very sorrowful with the weight of the world on his shoulders. The disciples were tired, but Jesus asked Peter, James, and John to watch. The disciples fell asleep. Jesus prayed. He returned to wake them. Then he went back to praying. Jesus returned again and asked, "Why are you still sleeping? It's time to get up. Here they come to get me."

1. Why do you suppose they spent their nights on the Mount of Olives?

2. Why do you think Jesus felt like he was under so much pressure?

3. Who do you think Jesus was praying for?

4. What would you have done if Jesus asked you to keep watch?

Ear cut off

John 18:1-11; Luke 22:49-51

Peter had one of the swords the disciples brought with them. When they came to arrest Jesus, Judas betrayed the Son of Man with a kiss. Peter sized up the situation. They were coming for Jesus. Judas had brought the high priest, and the high priest had brought the soldiers. Peter drew a sword and went toward the high priest. Then Peter cut off the right ear of Malchus, the servant who was with the high priest. Jesus said, "Enough of this!" He healed the man's ear. Jesus said, "I'm not leading a rebellion. I was in the temple every day, and you never touched me."

1. If you were Peter, how would you have felt when you saw Judas betray Jesus?

2. Why do you think Peter would choose to defend Jesus with a sword?

3. What do you imagine Malchus thought when Jesus healed his ear?

4. Why do you suppose the high priest did not arrest Jesus in the temple?

Peter's denial

Matthew 26:69-75; Mark 14:66-72; Luke 22:54-62; John 18:15-27

After Jesus was arrested, Peter followed along behind. In the courtyard three times people said Peter was a follower of Jesus. Some said they had seen him with Jesus. Peter denied it each time. But when he spoke and cursed, they could hear Peter's Galilean accent. Then the rooster crowed, just as Jesus had predicted. After that, Jesus was crucified on the cross. Peter and the other disciples fled, but John remained with Mary. Jesus died. They buried him in a tomb owned by Joseph of Arimathea.

1. Why do you think Peter followed along behind Jesus?

2. Why do you think they accused Peter of being a Jesus follower?

3. How do you think Peter felt when he heard the rooster?

4. Why do you suppose that Peter was nowhere to be found at the crucifixion of Jesus?

Prayer concerns

Prayer

Dear Lord Jesus,

Thank you for suffering on my behalf. Thank you for dying on the cross for my sins.

I cannot hide from you. You know my future. You know my inner faults and my selfishness.

Forgive me for the times that I ignore you. Forgive me when I take you for granted.

Help me to speak for you this day.

Amen.

1. Why do you suppose these women brought spices to the grave?

2. How do you think the women planned to get inside the tomb?

3. Why do you think the angel singled out Peter?

4. Why do you imagine that Jesus appeared first to Mary Magdalene?

Peter ran to the tomb

John 20:1-9; Mark 16:9-11; Luke 24:9-12; Matthew 28:11-15

The women hurried to find the disciples. In the meantime the soldiers reported to the chief priests what had happened. They all decided to make up a story that the disciples had stolen his body in the night. When Mary Magdalene and the other women told the Eleven that the tomb was empty, the disciples did not believe them. But Peter got up and ran toward the tomb. John followed and outran Peter. When John got there, he waited. Peter arrived and went inside ahead of John. The grave clothes were there but not Jesus. Then they remembered that Jesus had to rise from the dead.

1. What do you suppose the chief priests thought when the soldiers told them of the empty tomb?

2. Why do you imagine that the disciples did not believe what the women said?

3. Why do you think John waited for Peter to arrive?

4. If you were Peter, what would you be thinking when you went to the tomb?

Jesus appeared

Luke 24:13-49; Mark 16:12-14; John 20:19-23; 1 Corinthians 15:5

After the resurrection, Jesus appeared to Peter. On Easter Sunday night the disciples were behind locked doors. Jesus appeared in the room and bid them "Peace be to you." They thought he was a ghost, so Jesus said, "Touch me. See I have flesh and bones. I'm not a ghost. Do you have anything to eat?" They gave him some fish. But Thomas wasn't at that meeting. He doubted what they told him. Later Jesus appeared to more than 500 of the brothers at the same time. He also appeared to James. A week later they were back in the house locked in the room. Again Jesus appeared. He insisted that Thomas touch him. Jesus said, "You believed because you saw. Blessed are the people who believe when they cannot see me."

1. Why do you suppose the disciples were meeting behind locked doors?

2. If you were one of the disciples, how might you react when you saw Jesus?

3. Why do you think he appeared to James separately?

4. Why do you think that Thomas doubted when the rest of the disciples believed?

Peter went fishing

John 21:1-14

After Jesus appeared to the disciples in Jerusalem, Peter and the disciples went to Galilee. One night they went out to fish. Early in the morning, a man called asking if they had caught anything. They answered, "No." Then the man told them to throw their net on the right side of the boat. They did so and caught 153 fish. When he saw that the man was Jesus, Peter put more clothes on. Then Peter jumped in the water and made his way to shore. The boats followed. Jesus had built a fire. He asked for some fish and cooked breakfast for them. Jesus ate bread and fish with the men.

1. Why do you think the disciples went to Galilee?

2. If you were Peter, why would you go back to fishing?

3. Why do you suppose Peter got dressed when he saw Jesus?

4. Why do you think it is significant that Jesus ate bread and fish with them?

Peter's death foretold

John 21:15-25

After breakfast, Jesus asked Peter three questions followed by three commands. Each was a variation of: "Do you love me? Then feed my flock." The first question was, "Do you love me more than these?" Each time Peter said that he did. The first time Jesus commanded him, "Feed my lambs." Then he asked, "Simon son of John" (a variation on the name Jonah), "do you love me? Then shepherd my sheep." The third time the command was, "feed my sheep." Jesus told Peter that when he was old, he would be led about and be dressed by others. Peter would have his hands stretched out and die in a manner that glorified God, implying crucifixion. Peter asked, "What about John?"

1. How do you think it was significant that Jesus asked Peter "Do you love me?" three times?

2. What do you think Jesus meant by the phrase "love me more than these?"

3. What do you think the words "feed my sheep" mean?

4. Why do you think Peter asked about what would happen to John?

Ascension of Jesus

Acts 1:3-11; Luke 24:50-53

Jesus had told his disciples he would be returning to heaven. Then he would send the Holy Spirit. They were not to leave Jerusalem until the Holy Spirit came to baptize them. Forty days after his resurrection, Jesus took his followers up the Mount of Olives. They stopped in the area of Bethany. Jesus lifted his hand and blessed them. While they watched, Jesus was taken up into heaven. A cloud hid him from their sight. As they peered into the sky, two men dressed in white (described like angels) stood among them. They addressed the group. "Men of Galilee, why are you looking up into the sky? This same Jesus will return the same way you saw him go." With great joy they returned to Jerusalem. Every day they worshipped Jesus in the temple, praying and praising God.

1. How prepared do you expect they were to have Jesus leave them?

2. What do you suppose they thought when Jesus was taken up in a cloud?

3. Why do you imagine they referred to the group as "Men of Galilee"?

4. If you were Peter, what would motivate you to worship daily at the temple?

Prayer concerns

Prayer

Our Father in Heaven,

I praise you for your power. Thank you for raising Jesus Christ from the dead to live forevermore.

Today I celebrate your presence in my life. I look for evidence of you working around me and in me.

Forgive me for my sins. As you gave Peter another chance, make me who you want me to be.

Renew my love for you and for your people.

In your name I pray.

Amen.

Chapter 5 - Church launch

Matthias chosen

Pentecost sermon

Crippled beggar

Preaching to onlookers

Peter and John arrested

Prayer meeting

Ananias and Sapphira

Peter's shadow

Apostles arrested

Matthias chosen

Acts 1:12-26

After Jesus ascended up into heaven, they returned to Jerusalem. It was about an hour's walk away, about the distance one was allowed to walk on a Sabbath day. Peter returned with the group to the upstairs room where they were staying. At one point he spoke about Judas and how his act of betrayal and death were foretold in the Psalms. Then Peter added that they needed to choose a new disciple. They came up with two possible replacements and prayed about the decision. Then they cast lots. The choice fell to Matthias.

1. What do you suppose they talked about on the way back to Jerusalem?

2. How do you presume Peter knew about the betrayal from the Psalms?

3. What impresses you about the way Peter demonstrated leadership?

4. What do you think about the method used to select Matthias?

Pentecost sermon

Acts 2:1-41

The believers were all together on the day of Pentecost when the Holy Spirit enabled them to speak in tongues. Foreigners who were visiting from other countries were able to understand in their own language what the believers said. Then Peter stood up and preached to the gathering crowd. He reminded them of the prophecy Joel gave concerning the Spirit, signs, and wonders. Peter pointed to Jesus Christ who was crucified and raised from the dead. He had witnessed those events. Peter challenged the listeners to repent and be baptized. Three thousand people responded to his invitation. The revival lasted for many days.

1. Why do you think the Holy Spirit enabled them to speak in tongues?

2. Do you think that speaking in tongues today differs from Pentecost?

3. What do you think about the sermon Peter preached?

4. What impact do you imagine this revival had on the early church?

Crippled beggar

Acts 3:1-10

Peter and John went up to the temple for afternoon prayers. Everyday someone placed a man near the temple gate called Beautiful so he could beg. This man was born crippled and could not walk. When the man asked for money Peter said, "Look here. I don't have silver or gold, but I will give you what I do have. In the name of Jesus Christ of Nazareth, get up and walk." Peter grabbed the man's right hand and picked him up. Immediately the man felt strength in his feet. He jumped, and walked, and praised God in front of everyone. Then the man accompanied Peter and John into the temple. People who recognized the man were amazed.

1. Why do you think it is good to have a regular time for prayer?

2. What would motivate you to help a handicap person?

3. Why do you suppose beggars line up outside the temple gate?

4. If you were Peter, why would you be certain that the man would be healed?

Preaching to onlookers

Acts 3:11-26

When Peter healed the crippled man the crowds watching were astounded. Word quickly spread and people came running. Then Peter took the opportunity to speak of Jesus. "Why do you act as if we healed this man in our own power?" Peter said that the spiritual giants of old, men like Abraham, Moses, and Samuel, were looking for the Messiah. Jesus is that Messiah. Right there in the temple Peter said, "Jesus came to you. And you handed him over to Pilate to be killed. God raised Jesus from the dead. Now he gives you this opportunity to turn from your wicked ways."

1. Why do you think people are amazed when God performs a miracle?

2. Why do you expect this was a great opportunity for Peter to preach?

3. What impresses you about the content of Peter's message?

4. How do you imagine people in the temple reacted to accusations of having Jesus killed?

Peter and John arrested

Acts 4:1-22

The priests, the captain of the temple guard, and the Sadducees had Peter and John seized. They put the two men in jail for preaching in the temple. By now there was a following of five thousand believers. The next day the Sanhedrin brought Peter and John in to be questioned. Peter talked to them about how Jesus was raised from the dead and about salvation in the name of Jesus. The religious leaders noted that Peter and John were just ordinary uneducated men who had been with Jesus. Then the Sanhedrin commanded them to stop teaching about Jesus or preaching in his name. But Peter and John said they had to obey God rather than men. The Sanhedrin threatened them further and let them go. They didn't dare detain the men again because everyone knew the man who was healed had been crippled for over forty years.

1. What do you imagine Peter and John were thinking that night in jail?

2. How do you think the people reacted to their arrests?

3. What qualities about Peter and John do you think made them special?

4. What authority do you assume the Sanhedrin expected to have?

Prayer meeting

Acts 4:23-31

When they were released, Peter and John went back to their church group. They told their friends what happened to them before the Sanhedrin. In response the believers held a prayer meeting. They praised God for His mighty works in the days of David. They recounted the manner in which Herod and Pontius Pilate had treated Jesus. It was all part of God's plan. The believers sought help in view of the threats they faced. They asked that the Lord would enable them to speak God's word with boldness, and that he would perform miraculous signs. Suddenly the meeting place shook. They were all filled with the Holy Spirit and spoke the word of God with boldness.

1. If you had been Peter, how do you think you would have reacted when you were released?

2. What types of things do you observe that they prayed about when they met?

3. What do you think they expected the Lord to do in the near future?

4. What kind of help do you see them requesting for themselves?

Ananias and Sapphira

Acts 5:1-11

Some believers sold property or possessions and gave the proceeds to the church. The money was used to support those in need. Ananias and Sapphira sold property and lied saying they gave all the money to the church. Peter said they could have done whatever they wanted with their own property or money. Then Peter added, "You have not lied to men but God." With this, Ananias dropped dead. When his wife Sapphira arrived, she gave the same story as her husband. Then she also dropped dead. This scared the whole church.

1. What do you think motivated the believers to give to the church?

2. How do you imagine the poor reacted to the help the church gave them?

3. Why do you think that Ananias and Sapphira lied?

4. What do you imagine made the whole church afraid when the lying couple dropped dead?

Peter's shadow

Acts 5:12-16

The apostles performed many signs and wonders. The believers met regularly in the temple at Solomon's Colonnade. People respected them, but they were afraid to join them in the temple. Still, the total numbers of believers grew daily. Stories about Peter spread so that people flocked to be near him. They knew he would be walking by on his way to the temple, so they laid sick people on cots and mats along the streets. They hoped that Peter's shadow might fall on some of them as he passed by, and then the sick would be healed.

1. Why do you imagine some people were afraid to meet in the temple?

2. Why do you think they added so many new believers?

3. Who do you suppose would put a sick person on a bed in the street?

4. How sick does a person need to be before you ask God for healing?

Apostles arrested

Acts 5:17-42

The Sanhedrin had the apostles rearrested and put them in jail. During the night an angel broke them out of jail and told them, "Go stand in the temple courts and tell people the words of this life of faith." The next morning the Sanhedrin sent to the jail for the apostles, however they found that the jail was locked but empty. Then someone told the Sanhedrin that the apostles were preaching in the temple courts. The captain and officers brought them back to the Sanhedrin without using force. Again the Sanhedrin ordered them not to teach in the name of Jesus. Peter and the other apostles replied, "We must obey God rather than men."

1. Why do you think the Sanhedrin had the apostles rearrested?

2. If you were Peter, what would you be thinking when an angel got you out of jail?

3. What difference do you notice the second time the apostles were brought before the Sanhedrin?

4. In what situation might you choose to obey God rather than men?

Prayer concerns

Prayer

Dear Jesus,

You are the savior of the world. You have always been God's plan to reach me. Thank you.

I believe you died on the cross to pay for my sin.

I believe you rose from the dead.

I turn from my sins and choose to follow you.

I commit my life to you.

Show me the power of your Holy Spirit in my life.

In your name I pray.

Amen.

Chapter 6 - Church outreach

Preaching in Samaria

Paul meets Peter

Aeneas at Lydda

Dorcas at Joppa

Cornelius at Caesarea

Peter criticized

Prison escape

Council at Jerusalem

Preaching in Samaria

Acts 8:14-25

Saul and others were persecuting the church continually. The apostles stayed in Jerusalem, but most of the other disciples fled, taking the message of Jesus with them. Philip preached in the villages of Samaria and many believed. Then the apostles in Jerusalem sent Peter and John to Samaria to check it out. The two prayed with new believers. When Peter and John laid hands on them, these new believers received the Holy Spirit. Simon the sorcerer was impressed. Simon offered money to buy the Holy Spirit, but Peter rebuked him. Then Simon asked for prayer. After this Peter and John preached the gospel in many Samaritan villages as they worked their way back to Jerusalem.

1. How do you suppose persecution helped the early church to grow?

2. If you were Peter, what would you be thinking on your way to check out the new believers?

3. Why do you think that receiving the Holy Spirit was significant?

4. Why do you suspect that Simon the sorcerer thought he could offer money?

Paul meets Peter

Acts 9:26-30; Galatians 1:18

Saul planned to capture Christians, but the Lord interrupted Saul on the road to Damascus. After his conversion, Saul became known as Paul. He went to Jerusalem to join the disciples. Paul stayed with Peter for 15 days. He met James who was the head of the church in Jerusalem. (This James was probably the brother of Jesus and of Jude and the writer of the book of James.) The other disciples did not meet with Paul, because they were afraid of him. Previously, Paul had tried to imprison or kill the believers. But now the Jews tried to kill Paul, so the church sent him off to Tarsus.

1. Why do you suppose Paul would want to meet with the church leaders in Jerusalem?

2. If you were Peter, why would you be receptive to Paul?

3. Why do you think the disciples were afraid of Paul?

4. What do you think would motivate the Jews to be out to kill Paul?

Aeneas at Lydda

Acts 9:32-35

For a while things stabilized. The church continued to grow in peace under the fear of the Lord and the comfort of the Holy Spirit. Peter left Jerusalem and traveled down to Lydda to visit the believers. This place was on the road to Joppa. There, in the town of Lydda, he found a man named Aeneas who was paralyzed and lying on a bed for eight years. Peter called the man by name and then told him, "Jesus Christ heals you. Get up and make your bed." Aeneas got up. The people who saw the miracle turned to the Lord.

1. If you were Peter, why would you want to visit believers in other towns?

2. Why do you suppose the apostles seemed to find the sick wherever they went?

3. How do you think Peter knew the name of the paralyzed man?

4. How do you imagine the local people reacted to the healing of the paralyzed man?

Dorcas at Joppa

Acts 9:36-43

Along the Mediterranean Sea in the town of Joppa was a woman named Tabitha (in Aramaic), whom the Greek speaking people called Dorcas. She was very kind and always helped the poor. One day Dorcas became sick and died. Since Peter was in nearby Lydda, two men went to get him. They urged Peter to come quickly. When Peter arrived in Joppa, people showed him clothes that Dorcas had made for them. Her body was upstairs. Peter prayed for her and said, "Tabitha, get up." She opened her eyes, saw Peter, and sat up. He helped her to her feet. Many people believed in the Lord. Peter stayed there a while with Simon the tanner.

1. Why do you think people cared so much about the woman called Dorcas?

2. Why do you suppose the people of Joppa decided to go get Peter?

3. If you were Peter, what would you think when you learned about Dorcas?

4. What impact do you imagine her healing had on those in Joppa?

Cornelius at Caesarea

Acts 10:1-48

God appeared in a vision to the Roman centurion Cornelius at Caesarea. He told Cornelius to send men for Peter. So Cornelius sent servants down the coast toward Joppa. The next day at noontime Peter had a vision that the Lord told him to eat unclean animals. Peter refused. God said these animals were now clean. As Peter pondered this, the servants from Cornelius showed up. Peter traveled with them north to Caesarea. When he got there, Peter realized that this Gentile was neither Jewish nor from Palestine. Yet Cornelius had put his faith in Jesus Christ. Because of this Peter realized that God does not show favoritism but accepts people from anywhere as believers. Later Cornelius was baptized.

1. Why do you think it was significant that a vision came to Cornelius?

2. What affect do you think Peter's vision about animals has on what we eat today?

3. If you were Peter, how would you react to the men who came from Cornelius?

4. What do you think Peter discovered by dealing with Cornelius?

Peter criticized

Acts 11:1-18

The Jewish believers heard that the Gentiles had received the word of God. Some criticized Peter for his involvement with Cornelius. Those complainers thought that all believers should become circumcised, like any Jewish man would be. So Peter went up to Jerusalem to explain the situation to the apostles and other leaders. Peter told them the story of the vision he saw about unclean animals. He found that Cornelius and his household had repented and turned to God. Peter explained that God gave Cornelius and his household the same gift of the Holy Spirit that they all had. To oppose them would be to oppose God. Peter's explanation satisfied the church leadership.

1. Why do you suppose the believers in Jerusalem were upset with Peter?

2. If you were Peter, how would you feel about having to explain yourself to the church?

3. What do you think was the spiritual significance they placed in circumcision?

4. Why do you imagine it was hard for the church leaders to argue with Peter's explanation?

Prison escape

Acts 12:1-19

James the brother of John was put to death by Herod. This pleased the Jews, so Herod had Peter arrested too. The church prayed for him. The night before Peter's trial, an angel broke him out of prison. The angel told him to get up and get dressed. The chains fell off, and the gates opened. The angel left him in the street. So Peter went to the home of Mary, the mother of Mark. Peter knocked on the door. A servant girl named Rhoda heard his voice and told those praying that Peter was outside. They brought him in. He told them to tell James the head of the church about how an angel brought him out of the prison.

1. What do you think made James the brother of John such a significant person to put to death?

2. Why do you think the Jewish leaders were happy that James was put to death?

3. If you were Peter, how would you feel about your escape from prison?

4. What do you suppose they were praying about at Mary's home?

Council at Jerusalem

Acts 15:1-21; Galatians 2:7-9; James 1:1; Jude 1:1; Matthew 13:55; Mark 6:3

Some in Antioch taught that all believers needed to be circumcised in line with the teaching of Moses. Others taught that Gentile believers do not need to be circumcised. Paul and Barnabas were appointed to go to Jerusalem, because that church had dealt with this issue years before. James, Peter and John received Paul and Barnabas favorably. Peter spoke to the church that his primary ministry was to the Jews, but their primary ministry was to Gentiles. Therefore they should not force Gentile believers to be circumcised. James the head of the church in Jerusalem agreed with Peter. They drafted a letter of instruction for the Gentile believers in Antioch. They also sent Judas and Silas to confirm verbally what the Jerusalem church had written. This Judas (Jude in English) was possibly the son of Mary, the brother of James and also the brother of Jesus.

1. Why do you think the church at Antioch argued over circumcision?

2. Why do you suppose Paul and Barnabas were the ones selected to go to Jerusalem?

3. What type of reception do you imagine the Jerusalem church gave them?

4. Why do you suspect Judas and Silas were sent along with a written letter?

Prayer concerns

Prayer

Dear Lord,

You showed your love for the whole world. You gave your life for all who believe.

Give me eyes to see people who need to come to faith in Jesus Christ. I pray for them.

Help me to be a good friend to those in my church family. Lead me to serve you faithfully.

Fill my mouth with words of blessing. Work in the lives of those that I love. Lead them to faith in you.

Amen.

Chapter 7 - New Testament books

1 Corinthians

1 Peter

2 Peter

1 Corinthians

1 Corinthians 1:12; 3:22; 9:5; 15:3-9

Each minister or missionary, each pastor or evangelist, each preacher or teacher has their own style and approach to serving God and reaching people. In New Testament times, some believers preferred Peter or Apollos rather than Paul. One thing that made Peter different than Paul was that Peter took his wife along with him. Chapter 15 tells of many to whom Jesus appeared after his resurrection, such as Peter, the Twelve, James, the apostles, and later, Paul.

1. Why do you think each person in ministry must have their own approach?

2. If you were Peter, how would you deal with the jealousy some had over Paul?

3. How well do you think Peter's wife knew Jesus?

4. What impact do you think a wife has on a man's ministry?

1 Peter

1 Peter 2:4-8; 2:21; 5:13; Galatians 2:7-9

In his first biblical letter, Peter wrote to believers scattered across Asia Minor, (modern day Turkey) including the Galatians. In part this is the same audience that James wrote to in his epistle. Peter wrote that though they had not seen Jesus, they believe in him. They come to Jesus as the living stone, a precious cornerstone that the builders rejected. Jesus is a stone that causes men to trip and a rock that makes them fall. These believers suffered many persecutions for their faith in Jesus Christ. Peter charged them to consider this. Christ suffered for them, leaving an example that they should follow in his steps. Peter also writes about how husbands and wives should treat each other. At the end of the book Peter mentions Silas and wrote about the man who wrote the gospel of Mark. Peter refers to Mark as his son.

1. Why do you think it was significant that Peter mentioned these believers had not seen Jesus?

2. Why do you think Peter wrote about Jesus as a stone or rock?

3. Why do you think Peter chose to write about husbands and wives?

4. Why do you suppose Peter treated Mark as a son?

2 Peter

2 Peter 1:12-21; 3:15; Acts 15:32; Jude 1:1

Peter tells believers that he did not make up stories about Jesus. Peter affirms that he and other gospel writers were eyewitnesses of these events. The writers of Scripture spoke from God as they were led by the Holy Spirit. The New Testament book of Jude is quoted almost completely in 2 Peter 2. The two men knew each other and one most likely quoted the other. It is clear from other passages that Peter was close to all the church leaders, such as James, Jude, Silas, John, Mark, Barnabas, and Paul. Peter calls him our dear brother Paul. He says that Paul writes the same way in all his letters using godly wisdom. Peter notes that some things Paul writes are hard to understand. Those who twist Paul's words do so at their own peril.

1. Why do you think it is significant that Peter was an eyewitness?

2. If you were Peter, why would the reliability of Scripture be important to you?

3. What kind of impact to you think church leaders have on each other?

4. What do you suppose Peter thought about Paul's letters?

Prayer concerns

Prayer

Father God,

You gave your son Jesus Christ for me. You offer me comfort through the Holy Spirit.

You teach me through your written word the Bible. Make your word clear to my mind as I read it.

You give me friends in your church. Help me to be a friend and to love those who love you.

I praise you God for the great things you have done in my life. Forgive me of my sins.

Guide me to walk in your ways all the days of my life.

Amen.

Leader's Guide

Welcome to small group leadership! Small groups meet for a variety of reasons. Groups need leaders. If you leading a small group, praise God. You serve a vital function. Consider these questions.

What is the purpose of your group?

Your small group exists for one or more very good reasons. You benefit when you keep the purpose of your group clearly in mind. I list several options. Pick a primary one or come up with your own.

To lead new people to faith in Christ.

To build fellowship among believers.

To learn how to be a disciple of Jesus.

To enjoy a hobby with fellow believers.

To grow into a future church congregation.

To bring community to those who are alone.

To study the Bible and gain in knowledge.

To meet with others in similar life situations.

To pray for the needs of those you care about.

To provide opportunity for service projects.

Whom do you expect to be in your group?

Where do your people come from? Are they part of your church congregation? Are they people in a similar life situation? Are they co-workers? Are they the same gender or in the same age bracket? Do they live in the same community?

Does your group already exist? Is your group open to new members? Or is your group full? If you are the leader, you should know. If you are open to new members, how similar do they need to be to those already in your group?

Where do you meet?

People need to know where to find you. Small groups may meet at a church building, in a home, in a restaurant, at a business during breaks, after classes at school, or just about any reasonable place that people can carry on a conversation.

When do you meet?

Make sure your group members know what day you meet and for how long. Do you meet daily? Do you meet weekly? Regular meetings work best.

How do you lead a discussion?

Picture yourself in a meeting. One person does all the talking. Everyone else sits there quietly. Bored. Okay, that's not the goal. We want participation!

You as the leader can encourage your small group by promoting a balanced discussion. A study guide like this one is designed for conversation. Try this. Read the passage aloud. Ask the questions one at a time. Stop talking. Let others in your group talk.

Who reads the passage?

You can. Some people hate to read out loud. If all the people in your group are comfortable reading out loud, then you may take turns. If only some people like to read, you can ask for volunteers. You decide that. Make sure that whoever reads can be heard and understood by others in the group.

Who asks the question?

You can. It is easier for the leader to control the flow of the discussion if you ask the questions. But if you need to break it up, ask for help. "Can I have a volunteer to read the next question?" or "Would someone read question number 3 for us?"

What if no one will answer the question?

If people know, like, and trust you, they are likely to participate. If they have interest in the subject, they will want to add something to the discussion.

If they feel comfortable in the environment, they are more likely to share. Many people do not like silence. After the question is asked, stop talking. Wait a few moments. Usually someone will speak.

When is it your turn to answer the question?

If no one else has anything to say, then it is your turn. If you have something good to add, share it now. When you finish, ask if anyone else has something they would like to share.

If a question seems very personal or difficult, you may choose to go first to break the ice. When one person answers, it triggers ideas for other people. Be careful. Make sure you do not talk too much.

What if you cannot answer the question?

Then don't answer. You do not need to have all the answers. However, if you read the passage and all the questions in advance (before the meeting) you have more time to think up a good response.

What if someone won't stop talking?

You need talkers to have a conversation. Beware of the person who delivers a lengthy monologue for every question. That's not a discussion.

Talkers will talk. Let them at first. Eventually they will stop or at least need to breathe! Thank them and ask if anyone else has something to share.

If one person continues to dominate the replies to every question, and if it seems to bother others in your group, you can try this. "Let's let someone else answer this next question first."

How long should you spend on each question?

You and those in your group know, and even feel, how long a meeting should last. Stay on schedule. You need to keep moving on to the next question.

This book is designed to be covered over multiple meetings. Determine how much of the material you plan to cover each meeting.

If you operate on a time limit for the meeting, stop on time. You can add or skip questions. You can pick up next time where you left off this time.

Be a good leader. People will love you for it.

Acknowledgments

The front cover is a picture of the Sea of Galilee.

The design was provided by Angie of **pro_ebookscovers**

Bible translations and quotes from
http://biblehub.com

I thank Todd McGlinchey for reading this book and offering helpful suggestions.

Special thanks goes to my wife Julie Sawyer for her editorial work. Any mistakes in this book are solely the responsibility of the author.

About the Author

Tim Sawyer writes on religion, humor, travel, sports, chess, health, history, and prison. Before he retired Tim was a sports editor, insurance underwriter, church pastor, baseball chaplain, and classification officer. Now he writes.

Tim Sawyer Author Updates

The author invites you to sign up for his email list. Tim Sawyer talks about his life. He writes books on faith, fun, fiction and whatever interests him. He would love to keep in touch.

Please subscribe using the link below.

http://eepurl.com/bNnb1b

Before You Go

If you like this, leave a short review. It helps.

Sawyer Publications books:

When Hank Met Flo - Book 0.5 (ball game)

Hank & Flo On The Go - Book 1 (road trip)

Peter: A model for following Jesus (Bible)

amazon.com/author/timsawyer

Printed in Great Britain
by Amazon